Letterland

16 pages

Early Years Workbook 2

Letters: g-m

Name:

Find Golden Girl's letters in her garden. Make them green.

Write Golden Girl's letter here.

2

Circle the things that begin with
Golden Girl's sound.
Then join them to Golden Girl.

Gg

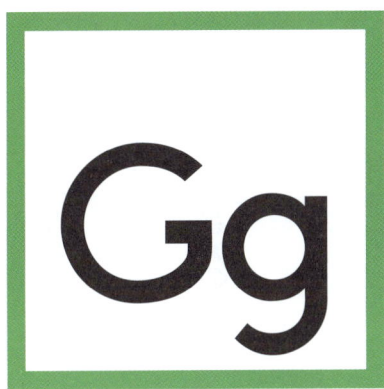

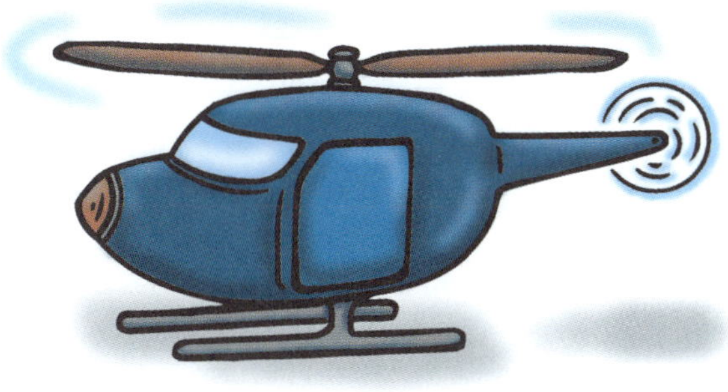

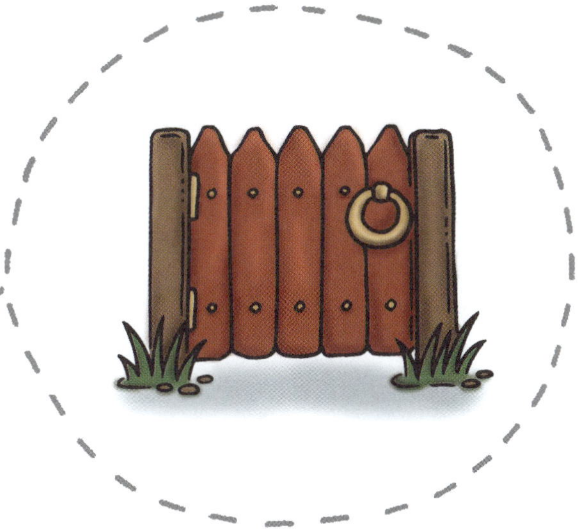

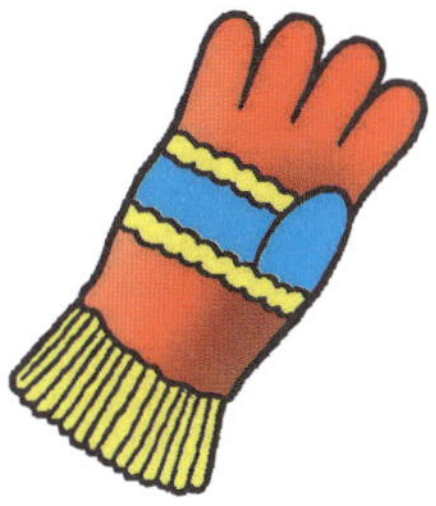

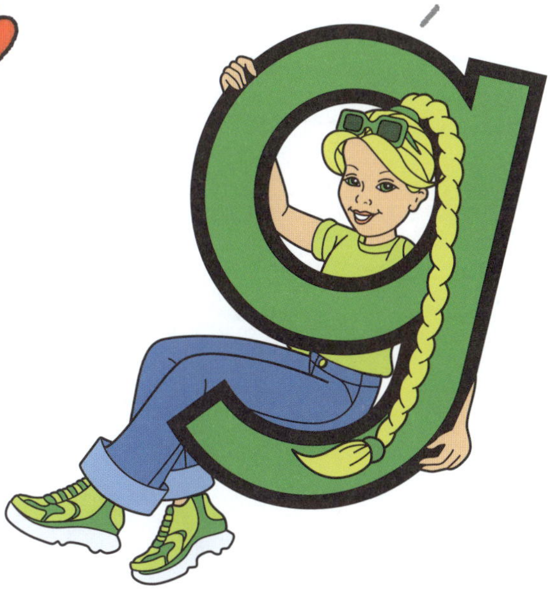

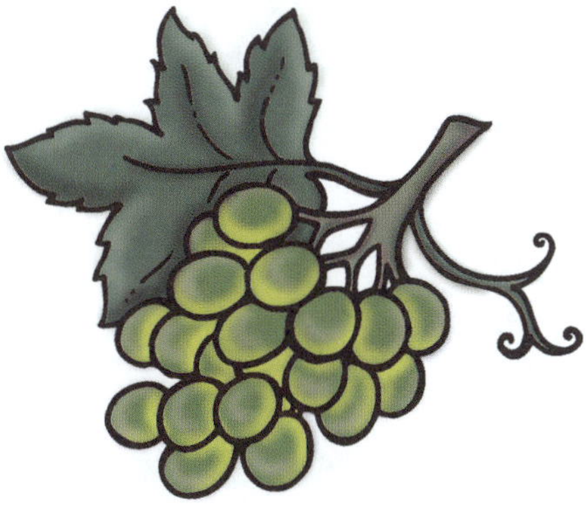

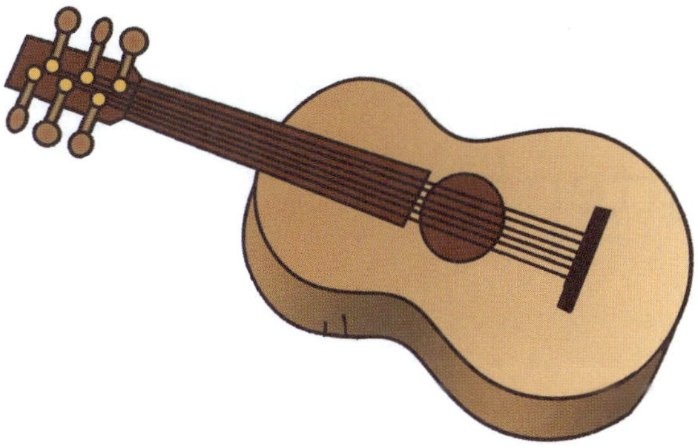

Look at Harry Hat Man's house. Find his letters. Then make the green.

Write Harry Hat Man's letter here.

What animal is Harry Hat Man holding in his hand? Join the dots and find out!

Draw something that makes you happy.

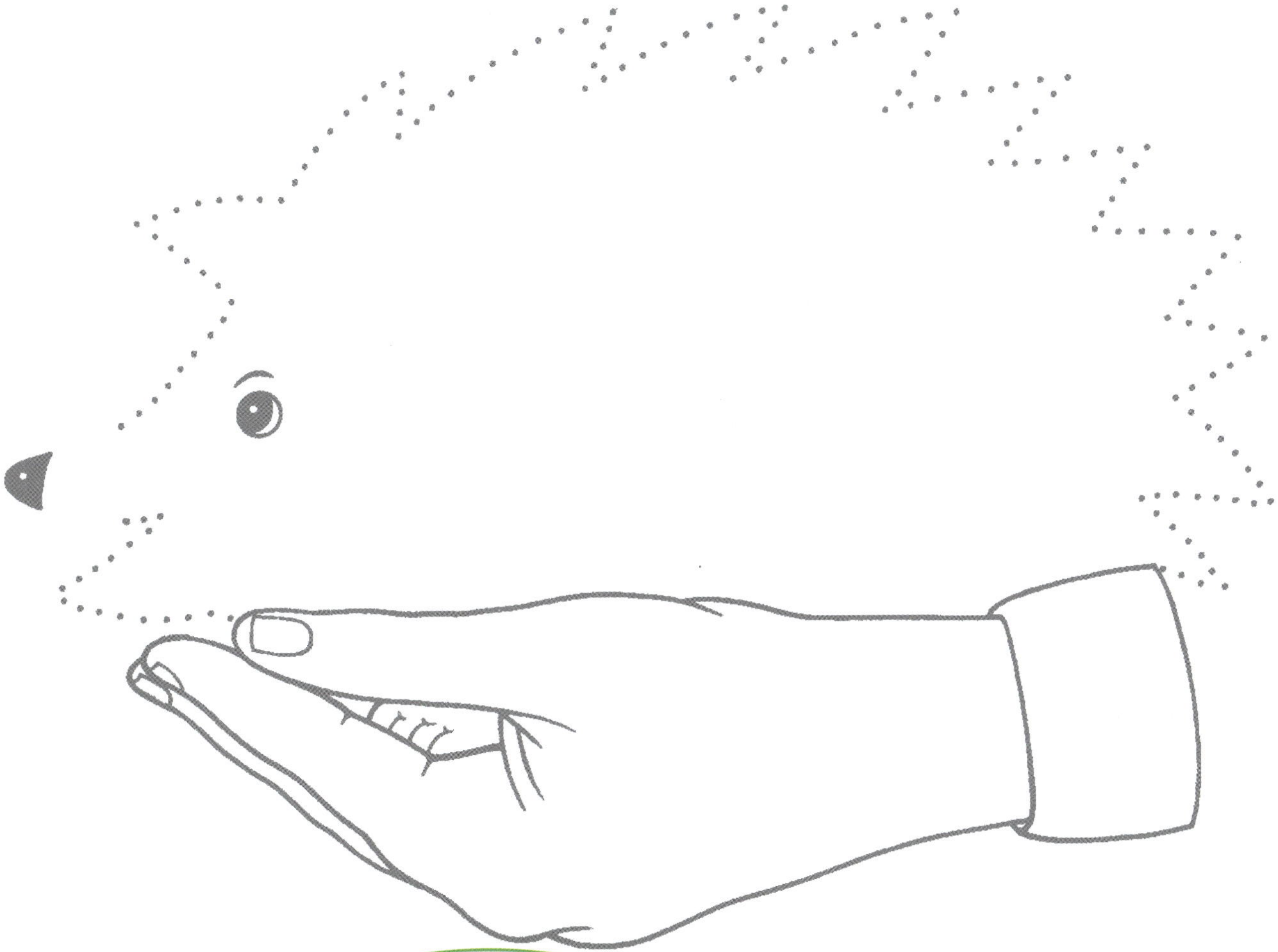

Find Impy Ink's letters in the sink. Make them yellow.

Write Impy Ink's letter here.

Cross out the picture that does not begin with Impy Ink's sound.

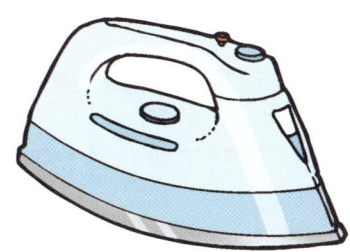

Sometimes I say my name in words. Listen for my sound in the things below.

Colour the jackets that have Jumping Jim's letter on them.

Write Jumping Jim's letter here.

Only one picture in each row begins with Jumping Jim's sound. Circle it.

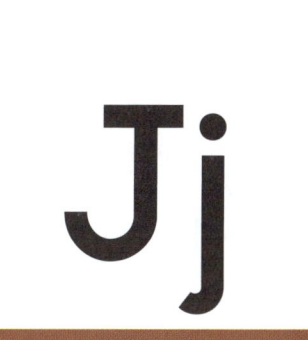

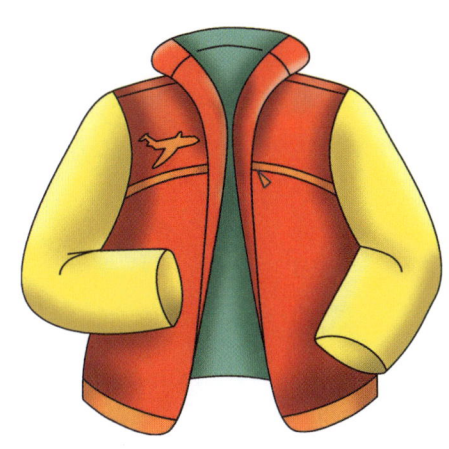

Can you find Kicking King's letters in his kitchen?
Make them blue.

Write Kicking King's letter here.

Follow the lines. Circle the things beginning with Kicking King's sound.

Kk

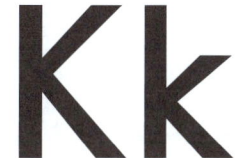

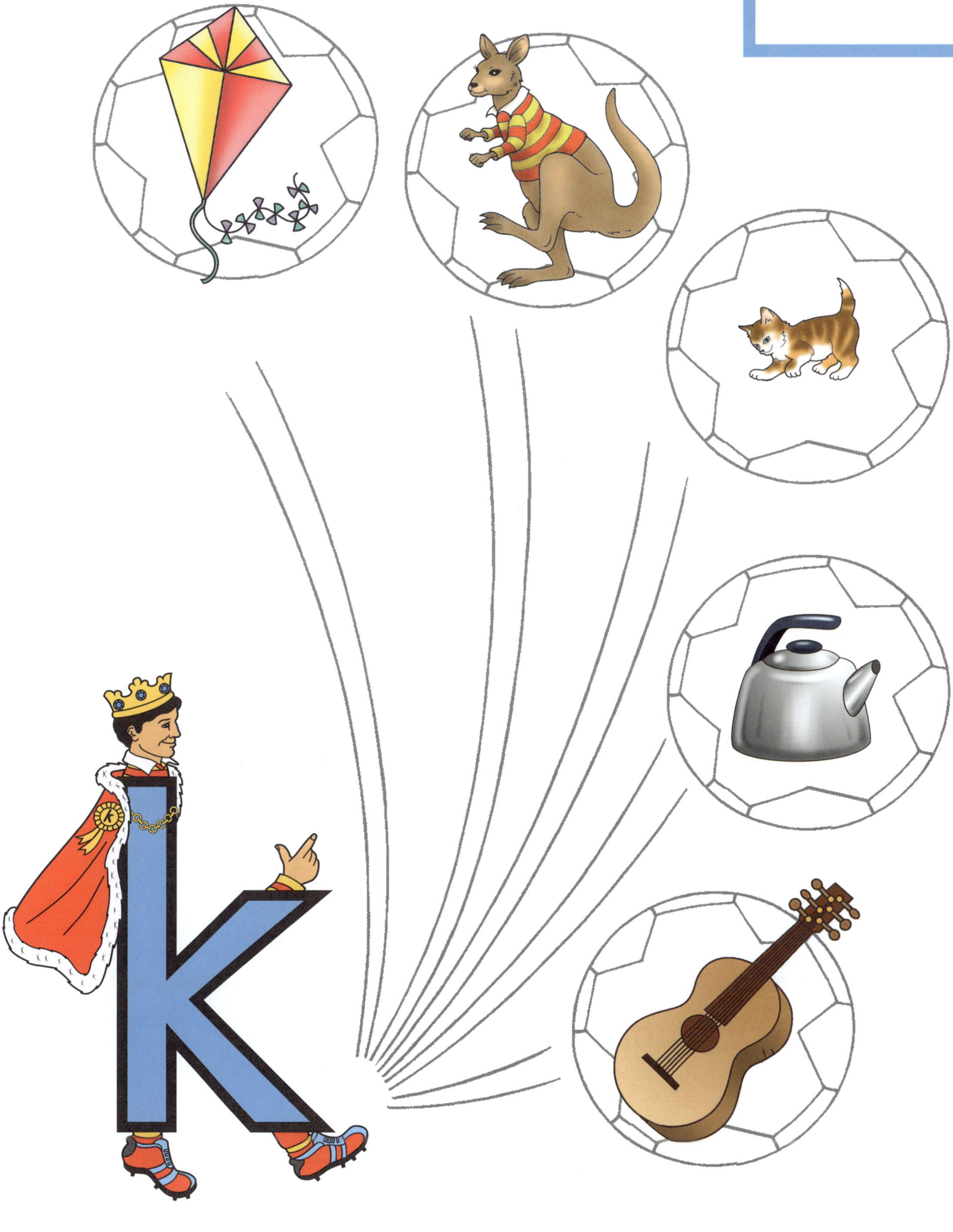

Look for Lucy Lamp Light's letters in the lampshade. Make them orange.

Write Lucy Lamp Light's letters here.

Look along this line of animals. How many begin with Lucy Lamp Light's sound? Colour them.

I can find ☐ animals that begin with Lucy's sound.

Now draw something long.

Look in the monster's mouth for Munching Mike's letters. Make them purple.

Write Munching Mike's letter here.

Colour the monster's mask.

Now think of something else that begins with Munching Mike's sound. Draw it in the box.

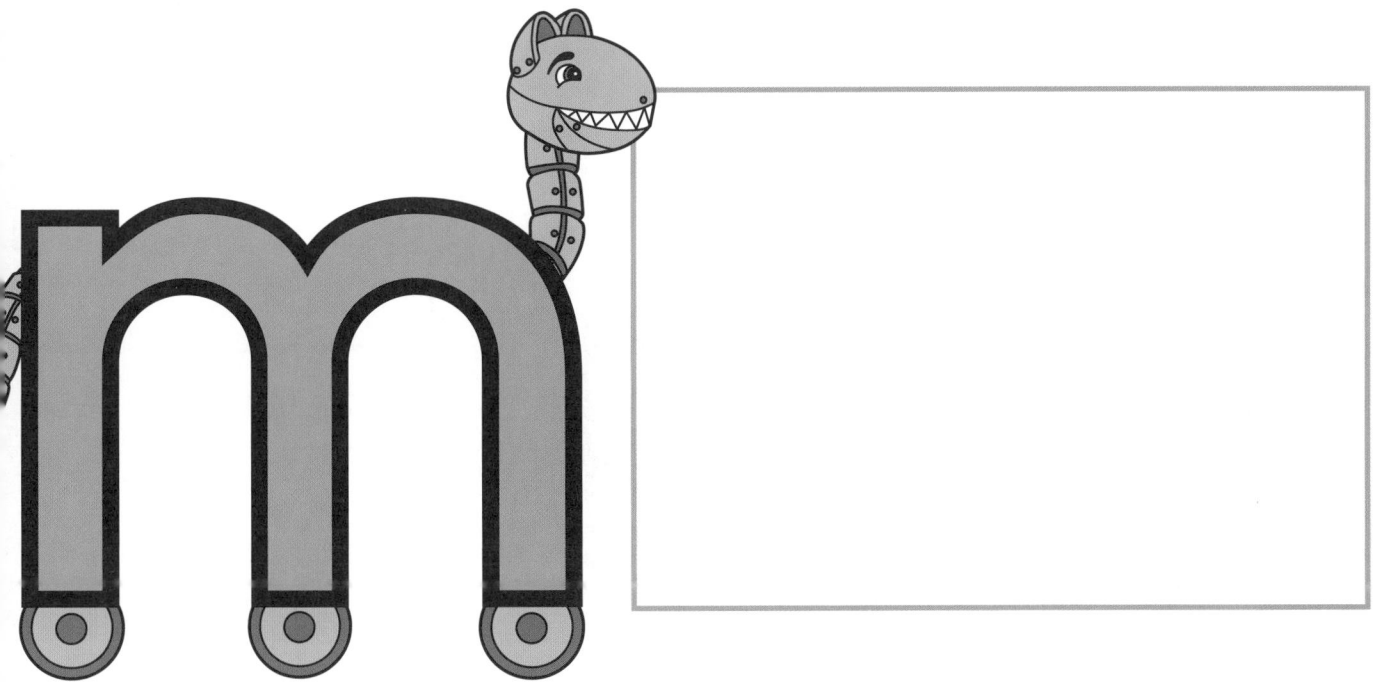

Look at the names under each picture.
Then draw the Letterlander.

Golden Girl

Harry Hat Man

Impy Ink

Jumping Jim

Kicking King

Lucy Lamp Light

Munching Mike

Published by Letterland International Ltd.
8/10 South Street, Epsom, Surrey, KT18 7PF, UK
© Letterland International 2006
ISBN: 978-1-86209-350-8

First published 1997.
This revised edition published 2006.
Reprinted 2008, 2011, 2012, 2014, 2018, 2020, 2021, 2023.
18 17 16 15 14

LETTERLAND™ is a trademark of Letterland International Ltd.

Written by Louis Fidge
Illustrated by Anna Jupp and Kathy Baxendale
Consultant: Lyn Wendon, originator of Letterland

All rights reserved. No part of this publication may be reproduced, stored in a retrieval system, or transmitted in any form or by any means, electronic, mechanical, photocopying, recording or otherwise, without the prior permission of the Publisher or a licence permitting restricted copying in the United Kingdom issued by the Copyright Licensing Agency Ltd, 90 Tottenham Court Road, London W1P 0LP.

British Library Cataloguing in Publication Data. A catalogue record for this book is available from the British Library.

Printed in Guangdong Province, China.

Code: T60
ISBN 978-1-86209-350-8

Letterland Child-friendly phonics